How Does My Home Work?
Electricity

Chris Oxlade

www.raintreepublishers.co.uk
Visit our website to find out
more information about
Raintree books.

To order:
☎ Phone 0845 6044371
🖷 Fax +44 (0) 1865 312263
✉ Email myorders@raintreepublishers.co.uk

Customers from outside the UK please telephone +44 1865 312262

Raintree is an imprint of Capstone Global Library Limited,
a company incorporated in England and Wales having its
registered office at 7 Pilgrim Street, London, EC4V 6LB
– Registered company number: 6695582

Edited by Daniel Nunn, Rebecca Rissman,
  and Catherine Veitch
Designed by Joanna Hinton-Malivoire
Picture research by Elizabeth Alexander
Production by Alison Parsons
Originated by Capstone Global Library Ltd
Printed and bound in China by Leo Paper Products

ISBN 978 1 406 23767 2
16 15 14 13 12
10 9 8 7 6 5 4 3 2 1

British Library Cataloguing in Publication Data
Oxlade, Chris.
Electricity. – (How does my home work?)
621.3-dc22
A full catalogue record for this book is available from
the British Library.

Acknowledgements
We would like to thank the following for permission
to reproduce photographs: Alamy pp. 8 (©
GraficallyMinded), 9 (© C J Wheeler), 16 (© Matthew
Kirwan); Corbis p. 20 (© Ocean); Shutterstock pp. 4
(© Harry Hu), 5 (© Jozef Sedmak), 6 (© yampi), 7
(© Monkey Business Images), 10 (© Mark William
Richardson), 11 (© Yegor Korzh), 12 (© Zeljko Radojko),
13 (© Tungphoto), 14 (© Yellowj), 15 (© Adrian Britton), 17
(© Mark Herreid), 18 (© Nick Hawkes), 19 (© anyaivanova),
21 (© Monika Wisniewska), 23 (© Yellowj, © THP | Tim Hester
Photography, © Harry Hu, © Monkey Business Images,
© Nick Hawkes, © Tungphoto, © Adrian Britton).

Cover photograph of an energy-efficient light bulb
reproduced with permission of Shutterstock (© Sideways
Design). Background photograph of vector lights
reproduced with permission of Shutterstock (© Kundra).

Back cover photographs of (left) a power station
reproduced with permission of Shutterstock (© Mark
William Richardson), and (right) a light bulb reproduced
with permission of Shutterstock (© Mark Herreid).

We would like to thank Terence Alexander for his invaluable
help in the preparation of this book.

Contents

Some words are shown in bold, **like this**. You can
find them in the glossary on page 23.

What is electricity?

Electricity makes lights and other things in our homes work.

Electricity is a kind of **energy**.

Most homes have electricity.

We can use electricity to make light, heat, and sound.

Where do we use electricity at home?

Electricity powers all sorts of machines in your home.

Can you name some of the machines electricity powers in this kitchen?

Electricity also powers many **gadgets** we use at home.

Electricity powers the control for this boy's games console.

Is electricity dangerous?

safety cover

Household electricity can injure or even kill a person.

Never play with electric plugs or **sockets**.

This is a special safety plug.

If anything goes wrong, the plug switches the electricity off.

Where is electricity made?

Some electricity is made at power stations like this one.

Power stations burn coal, oil, or gas to make electricity.

wind turbine

These machines are called wind turbines.

Wind turbines turn the **energy** from wind into electricity.

This is a hydroelectric power station.

The **energy** from water rushing downhill is turned into electricity.

power line

Electricity travels along **power lines** to towns and cities.

Cables under the street or on tall poles take the electricity to your home.

How does electricity get around my home?

Electricity travels around your home along wires and **cables**.

The wires and cables are buried in the walls and under the floors.

plug

socket

The cables carry electricity to **sockets**
in the walls.

To make a machine work you put its
plug into a socket.

How do electric lights work?

Cables carry electricity to the lights in your home.

Light switches turn the electricity to the lights on and off.

light bulb

A light bulb turns electricity into light.

When electricity flows into the bulb, the bulb glows brightly.

Does electricity harm our planet?

pollution

Burning materials such as coal, oil, and gas makes **pollution** in the air.

This causes a problem with our weather called **climate change**.

This power station makes electricity from sunshine instead.

This means we do not have to burn so much coal, oil, or gas.

How can we use less electricity?

We can help our planet by using less electricity.

For example, you can switch off lights when you do not need them.

Make sure your washing machine is full each time you use it.

Also, wash clothes at a lower heat to save electricity.

Saving electricity poster

Is your family good at saving electricity?

Make a poster to stick on your fridge, like this one, to remind people what to do.

How to save electricity

- Switch off the lights when you leave a room.
- Turn off the television when you are not watching it.
- Shut down the computer when you are not using it.
- Turn down the heating. Wear a jumper!
- Fill the washing machine up before you turn it on.
- Only boil as much water as you need.

Glossary

 **cable** tube with wires inside that carry electricity

 **climate change** when there is a change to normal weather conditions

 **energy** power that is needed to make things move, change, or grow

 **gadget** small machine

 **pollution** harmful things in the air, water, or soil. It is caused by humans.

 **power line** thick cable that carries electricity from a power station to homes

 **socket** special holes in the wall where you can plug in an electric machine

Find out more

Books

Electricity (Investigate), Chris Oxlade
(Heinemann Library, 2008)

Electricity (Popcorn: Science Corner), Angela Royston
(Wayland, 2010)

Websites

**www.engineeringinteract.org/resources/
siliconspies/flash/concepts/electricity.htm**
Play an interactive game about how we use
electricity, on this website from the University
of Cambridge.

www.switchedonkids.org.uk/
Find information about electricity supply and staying
safe with electricity on this website.

Index